Opalescence

A Rag-a-tag Ragbag of
Monsters, Ghosts and
Murders, Madness, Dances
and Dreams

Tim Hardy SSfB

Langley Press   Co. Durham

First published by the Langley Press, 2010
1ˢᵗ edition: #32/62

ISBN: 978-0-9544759-8-7

To Cate Wood and Pauline Callcott for their very-much-appreciated help starving the monster; to Dr Mercer for teaching me about patience and perseverance; and to Joanna Clark for reminding me about smiling.

Prefatory Note

A long, long time ago, my boss signed me up for the dictionary.com word of the day service. I expected to learn stuff, but they only supplied dull, real-dictionary explanations for the words they sent. In the spirit of Dingbatisation, I have blessed some of those words by defining their true meanings. These all-new, improved versions are included at strategic points throughout the book.

Acknowledgements

Thanks are due to a goodly number of people, diverse of both name and talent. In alphabetical order of contribution type:

Amy Barnes painted the beautiful **artwork** which graces the outside of this book.

Christine Jensen took the **author-photograph** displaying my **tattoo** in all its glory.

Robb Sutherland took the **author-photograph** in which I forgot to roll up my **trousers**.

Helen Tulloh wrote the **introduction** and proof read an early draft.

Jo Hill, Nigel King and Simon Webb all performed the unenviable task of **proof reading** various drafts, whilst Nigel and Simon further provided much-needed editorial assistance. Any 'errors' present in the final text have been inserted after editing, purely to annoy the pedantic.

Thank you all.

Contents

Word: *Woebegone* (proper n.):

In the little-known stories written by Prince Albert for his children, *Woebegone* was the name for a series of imaginary products which purported to do away with worry and strife but would always have hilariously unforeseen consequences.

The stories are collected in "*The Educational Tales of Walter and his Life of Woe*", a copy of which is available in the British Library.

Introduction

- *Helen Tulloh – Categorical Denier*

Tim is, as those who know him well, an all-round good egg and this project is driven by madness, imagination or simple faith. The first part of *Opalescence* blends personal experience with artistic licence, and we are privileged to be drawn into Tim's private world and to follow him on part of his spiritual journey. Read slowly and begin to catch a glimpse of Tim himself. Sometimes he is 'articulating the darkness'; sometimes he reveals God's unfailing light and love. And all this seasoned with humour. Tread softly...

The latter part embodies some of Tim's imaginative planning of activities accessible to groups of all ages. Give them a try and allow yourselves to be transformed.

Helen M. Tulloh

May 2010

The Mysterious Page X

Identity Theft (A Confession)

This isn't really being written by Tim.

I know his log-on details and passwords.
I know his bank details, where he works,
His car registration, birthday and mother's maiden name.

I know an awful lot about him:
The places he goes, the people he sees,
Those he loves and hasn't told,
Those he'd like to but won't tell.

I know what he did last summer.

But this isn't about Tim, it's about me:
The monster that lives in his head.

On a good day,
I confusticate, vex and confuddle him,
I could also m*ddle him
But the rhymes are saved for the last verse.

On a good day,
I help him forget,
I help him wish upon vain fancies,
And idly while-away the hours he could better spend.

On a good day,
I paint it black
In wondrous shades that hide the light:
A stormcloud in front of stars.

On a good day,
I don't have to do all that much -
The merest of whispers
and

He
almost
believes
he
is

me.

There's no room for a monster under his bed;
Tim's personal monster lives in his head.
I am Tim's monster and I want him dead.
But not yet(d).
I'm having far too much fun at the moment.

Tell your monster I said, "Hello."

The 31 Deaths of Evelyn Johnson:
An Introduction

It is a truth universally acknowledged[*] that amongst the almost-infinite number of parallel universes each of us will be born only thirty-one times. Generally, our parallel selves lead similar, if not identical, lives and although there may be some variation between parallels (freak accidents killing off two or three out of thirty one, for example), most of us will die old and in our beds.

Research has thrown up some anomalies.

Take the case of Bernie Rollins (b. 19th-24th August, 1942 d.18th June 1980-2003). This, otherwise remarkably dull, man is the only person in all history to have been killed by a falling, solid-gold piano thirty-one times. Once in each of thirty-one different cities, always on the 18th June but never on a Monday.

Or maybe that of Catherine Smith (b. 31st December 1977, d. 31st December 2008) who merits attention only for having been born on exactly the same day and having died on her thirty-first birthday in all of her thirty-one parallels.

However, my favourite of all the life and death studies I have come across so far, is that of Evelyn Johnson (b. 8th-21st April 1953, d. 5th June 1970 – 29th February 2028).

---

*Universally, that is, by the select small few who have done research into this matter and those who have read their papers. It's generally agreed that 'quantum' and 'probability' and (possibly) 'quantum probability' have something to do with it.

Although not much is known about her early life, the stories of her widely-varying deaths (collected here, and available to the public for the first time) are known. They make interesting, sometimes sad, sometimes humbling, sometimes entertaining reading. I hope getting to know Evelyn enriches your life as much as it has mine.

Professor John Ecclestone
International Parallels Research Centre, New Stafford.

Word: *Ostentation* (v.):

The act of running about in a wood in Germany looking for clues and symbols stapled to the sides of trees.

An (almost) Entirely True Story

I dough-nutted out last night.

Saw a box of mini chocolate dough-nuts just sitting on that
supermarket shelf.
They looked at me pleadingly:
"Rescue us from this dread place!"

I carried them away, away in a bag
Past the checkout
(there was a worrying moment when the assistant pointed an
infra-red gun at the box, but it passed).
Past the security guy
(security guys are just one step away from police-men – and
you know how they treat dough-nuts).
And past the giant double doors.
"Freedom!" I could hear them cheering,

To their horror,
I didn't release them into the vast wild plains where other
doughnuts dwell,
But ate them all up!
Gobble, gobble, gobble!

La Danse Macabre (pas)

There's a ghost, you won't have seen him, but he's there. All the time, he dances; every where he goes — always dancing. Dancing as if he didn't have a care in this world, or the next. Who knows? Maybe he doesn't.

What I do know is that he never stops dancing. Sometimes he dances slowly. Sometimes he dances fast. Sometimes it's the most most beautiful thing you ever saw (but you won't), as if he were dancing what a thousand hearts breaking for the love of the same woman all at once would feel like — sad, and lonesome, and somehow right at the same time. Sometimes, it's bad tap routines from hideous old black-and-white films, and you'd hope his ghostly tongue would be poked firmly into his ghostly cheek — it's hard to tell. But he's always dancing.

Always.

Some simple folks say that he's got dancin' feet, that it's the night fever, the light of the silvery moon, that he'll always be dancing and he always has. But he might not, and he hasn't.

Some slightly more together and knowledgeable types have been heard to say that it's true — the rhythm DID get him (but that's a joke that worked better when Chandler said it, and, besides, it's not even the half of it).

The truth of the matter is, pure and simple, the music took him. It took him and it never let him go.

All of his life, he had loved music.

Back when he was learning to crawl, he'd sit, transfixed, staring into the speaker of the radio his mother had playing in the background: as soon as the music started he would freeze where he was and stare at the source of the music; when it stopped, he'd turn away and his mind would move to other things, and when it began again, he'd snap back like a whip and stare deep into the speaker.

Of course, his mother fed his fascination. It kept him out of the way, and seemed to be stimulating his little brain. She quickly learned that it didn't matter what type of music was playing, as long as it played.

As he grew, he started trying to learn about music but had no aptitude for it whatsoever, which, rather than frustrating him, fascinated him all the more – how could something so foreign to his understanding affect him so deeply? All his spare time was spent reading about music; all his pocket money on tapes (and later, CDs and vinyl).

Briefly, he tried making friends with others who loved music, and hanging around with musicians, but this came to an end when he started to feel inferior – it was one thing not being able to make music or understand it himself, but quite another to listen to conversations about the thing he loved most and not be able to take part in any way. They aroused strange feelings of jealousy – these people who had a deeper relationship with the music that he loved than he ever could.

So he found a job at a record store and retreated behind the music he bought with his meagre earnings. Any time they wouldn't let him work – "You need some time off, we've got enough staff to cover the weekend, we're closed on Sundays," – he wandered around town listening to his music, getting more and more taken up in it as time went by.

He quit his job, resenting the interruptions that customers made on his listening schedule, moved back in with his mother who fed him and didn't talk any more, and walked around the town, listening to one of his two i-pods, carrying the other in case the first ran out of power half way through the day.

Every day he would listen, and every day he would become a little more frustrated – he knew he loved the music, but he couldn't understand any of it! He knew as much of the theory as anybody had any right to, and his head was full of crotchets and keys and scales, arpeggios, harmonies and dodgy middle eights, but he still didn't get it. It was driving him mad and he knew it, but he didn't know what he could do.

Some days he tried not listening at all, but after an hour or so, he couldn't cope any longer and back on went the headphones. He tried talking to people (with music on in the back ground, of course) but after the first, 'Hello's he'd drift away into the music and only notice that the other person had left when the CD needed changing. He couldn't make any progress, nor could he get away from the need to try.

It was driving him mad.

One day he was walking along the street, down by the old monument in town, when something distracted him. Some say it was a beautiful woman walking past and turning her head for a second glance. Some say it was the bleakness of the newspaper headline blowing around his feet. Some say it was the sheer joy and pleasure on the faces of two children chasing each other around about. Some say it was the pain as he stubbed his toe on a wonky paving stone. Some say it was a minor stroke, causing his brain to stop just for one moment. Others say that it's largely dependent on your definition of what music *is*.

It doesn't matter. That moment's distraction was all he needed. When his brain started again, everything fell into place, and for the first time in his life he found himself dancing, not just caught up in his head, but all of his being. And he couldn't stop. Throughout that afternoon, crowds gathered, some cheered, some danced with him, all went away tired as he carried on dancing. He danced all night and in the morning the crowds returned: as the novelty wore off, their enthusiasm at first cooled and then turned to derision. At some point, amongst the cat-calls and over-ripe fruit, he was mugged, and his i-pods with their precious music stolen, but the dance went on.

There's not much more to tell: how, to get away from the crowds and the jeers, he danced his way to the quiet places; how, one day, some kids, out for kicks, murdered him, their blows and stabs falling as his dance became ever more fluid and graceful – as if, with the blood and consciousness leaving him, the music took an even greater hold – and how his killers ran away screaming as he kept on dancing long after they'd spent their energies; how, after that, it was all a matter of time running its course and as the dance went on, his body drying out and shrinking until a skeleton in rags danced over the fields, scaring birds. Every so often, there would be a report of some drunken farmer being scared half to death by a dancing scarecrow.

Then, nothing. No trace was found of any remains. The music took him, utterly and completely. He danced until there was nothing left but the ghost of a dance.

And the dance goes on.

Word: *Deus ex Machina*

Not so much a word as a phrase. It is apparently derived from a modernist theory that says that God is Man's creation, but it wouldn't have been possible in the pre-industrial age, when men had no beliefs, morality or gods. The very concept of deity sprang wholly formed from the bowels of a factory which hitherto had been thought to be for the production of high quality runcible spoons.

George Eliot wrote about the "Deus ex Machina Incident" as it became known in her little-known tome "The Deus ex Machina Incident and its potential consequences for rural life".

Praying to a Silent God

Can someone tell me how to stop believing
In the silent, hidden deity
Who said, "I love you"
Once, so long ago,
Leaving
Me
A blind drunk,
Shadow boxing,
Lurching and screaming
At *his* demons?

Will no-one rid me of this troublesome
God?

Press Play Again

I would rip myself apart,
I would tear myself to shreds, and call it art.
There for all the world to see:
Exposed with no more secrets - me.
And I would **feel**.
Lying, I would call it art;
I would lie to all concerned.
It would not be art.
I would see the selfish act -
Achieving nothing, helping no-one.

Restraint is good, right?
Turn over.
Press play again.

A Story I Once Heard

I can't remember where I first heard this, but it's been doing the rounds for a good few years now – since well before any of the Ring films got made. There's not much to it really – just that a struggling young writer foolishly left his word-processor switched on when he went to bed having just watched *Naked Lunch*. He woke up in the morning to find that his keyboard had eaten half his lower left leg in the night. Some variations of the story say it was a wireless keyboard, but I believe the version which claims that the keyboard used its own cable as a make-shift tourniquet.

It's nearly time for bed now. To top off a day of film watching, I just watched *Naked Lunch*. My computer was switched on all the way through. In case it's got any ideas, I'll be switching it off at the wall and taking the batteries out of the wireless bits. But just in case, I'm posting this now so that you'll know if something happens to me tonight, so you'll know what it was – even though the authorities will try to hush it up.

Word: *Camarilla* (n.):

A female armadillo.

The Sign

"I was ever so proud of the new sign I had just bought. A metal plate with a hole to accommodate a screw at each corner and bearing the following in stark black capitals:

NO SALESMEN,
NO BEGGARS,
NO RELIGIOUS BODIES.

"Yes, it might be brusque to the point of rudeness, but I considered my time at home to be my own. I screwed the plate into position, just beside the door at shoulder height – where nobody could miss it. It seemed that my days of being woken at all hours by assorted ne'er do wells and do-gooders were coming to an end.

"The very next day I was woken up by an insistent ringing of the doorbell. All my friends know I work nights at this time of year so I knew there was either some emergency (I don't trust telephones and wouldn't dream of having one of those evil things in my house – if there's a problem at work or with my parents then one of my neighbours is happy to take the call and take a message (or, in the direst emergency, come and wake me up) or that somebody was rudely ignoring the sign. Bleary-eyed, I trundled down the stairs and opened the door. A forty year old creature stood before me. It was wearing an old brown suit so crumpled it was almost a cliché and holding a worn-looking brief case. It held out an ID card. It was a salesman!

"I glared and pointed at the sign. "That's why I'm here," it said, "It appears that somebody has unscrewed what is undoubtedly a very fine sign and replaced it face down. Kids these days!" It shrugged at me, trying to give the impression that this was something that happened regularly and I was the victim of a growing sign-turning epidemic. "I have the solution to your problem. Pete's Patented imPregnable Paste! Guaranteed to keep any two surfaces bonded together until one crumbles away. Only five pound a tin." It knelt down and opened the case and started rattling off some awful sales pitch which I tuned out; I'd seen the screw driver sticking out of its back pocket as it knelt down and recognised the car that it had obviously driven as one that can be seen perpetually in the car park outside the shop where I bought the sign, and it might have been my imagination, but it looked like there was a uniform for the store hanging in the passenger window. Admiring the cleverness, if nothing else, I interrupted, retreated indoors to pick up some cash and bought a tin – there was no way that sign was going to be moved again this side of eternity!

"Having replaced the sign I returned to my bed and slept soundly. Soundly that is until I was woken again by the doorbell. I crawled out of bed and down the stairs and opened the door expecting the worst. A filthy beggar was standing there. I pointed at the sign and saw the hideous mess the "glue" had made of the wall – it was as if concentrated acid rain had eaten away at the brick leaving a ragged impression where the sign had been. The sign lay face down on the ground. Before the beggar could start what was obviously going to be a drunken and long-winded appeal I told him to hold on a minute. I rummaged through my cupboards, found several tins of food, and a can opener, and a fork. I took these downstairs, grabbing my last five pound note and gave away the lot. Anything for a quiet day's sleep. I was desperate. The tramp went away with a huge smile on its face as I screwed the sign back into the wall above the crumbly bit. I returned to bed thinking that maybe charity wasn't such a bad thing after all.

"No sooner had my head hit the pillow than the door bell rang again. By this time I wasn't thinking straight and grabbed my grandfather's old service revolver in the hope that I could use it to scare away anybody who shouldn't be there. I opened the door and pointed straight away to the sign with the gun. Miraculously it was still attached to the wall and facing the right way. "Fuck your sign!" said one of the two conservatively dressed young men holding Bibles and Watchtower magazines. He grabbed the gun, I swear I didn't know it was loaded, and shot his partner point blank through the head before turning the gun on himself."

"No further questions, Your Honour."

Word: *Importunate* (adj.):

Strictly, lacking in portunance, but used more generally to describe a dearth of fortified wines in a drinks cabinet.

The 31 Deaths of Evelyn Johnson:
Number 7: Deus ex Machina

On the day Evelyn Johnson decided to kill herself (June 5th), the sun was shining, the birds were whistling (needless to say, in the trees), and, all around her, the world radiated a sense of all being well. Four weeks later, on the day she went through with her plan, the conditions remained pretty much as they had all summer.

She'd spent the month putting her affairs in order and had even changed her will to better represent her current relationships, loved ones and favourites. All her belongings were packed up and ready for distribution to various worthy causes and named individuals. Her fridge was empty, turned off at the wall and its door was open so that the world (with which all was well) could see the freshly-cleaned sparkle. Evelyn had paid her utilities bills until the end of the month, and informed her landlord that she would be moving out and that somebody would be along to pick up her stuff by the end of August. She'd even sent out a letter to all her friends, which explained clearly and succinctly what she would be doing and what the practical consequences were likely to be.

Evelyn walked calmly out of her flat, locked the door behind her and sealed the keys in an envelope which she posted to her solicitor at the first post box she passed as she went her not-so-merry way. After about a mile, she came to the highest bridge in the area, walked half way across, climbed over the side, and after a brief pause, leaned outwards and let go of the structure, whereupon she began to fall.

And falling is where we must briefly leave her.

Somewhere in the Amazon, God commanded an unseasonal butterfly to flap its wings twice as fast as it usually did for a moment or two. Chaos theory was kind-of validated, and we now return to Evelyn.

A very strong wind blew the falling would-be-suicide into the branches of a nearby tree, the branches broke her fall, gradually slowing her down until she tumbled gently from the lowest branches onto the ground below. Besides a slightly twisted ankle and the bruising sustained in the first impact with the tree, she was completely unharmed.

A voice rang out from the heavens, "Evelyn Johnson. Know that it is for God, not you, to choose the moment of your passing."

As Evelyn repented, vowing to make amends, God commanded a bolt of lightning…

Later that afternoon, council workers, investigating the unusual weather, discovered Evelyn's body. The lightning hadn't even touched her, having naturally struck the tallest object nearby – the tree. The tree had been split from top-most-tip to root, and then fallen both due east and due west. It was the half pointing towards Jerusalem that had fallen on Evelyn and squashed her flat.

Closer

"I love you, Tim." she said,
And I pulled her closer to me.
That night,
It was impossible to tell
Where I ended and she began.
It was just as hard to tell
Where the sex stopped and the tears started.

God was there, and
Understanding,
Wept too.

A Winter Invocation

At this time of cold and death,
At the sinking of the new moon,
The clearing of the sky of clouds,
The retreat of warmth from our world,
The freezing of our breath,
And the fading of the light from our eyes,
Be with us in these dangerous hours
That we may live again
To see new light and feel new warmth.

The Waiting Room

You are ushered into a comfortable waiting room with two huge, ornate lift-fronts at one end. There are rows and rows of chairs opposite the doors – full of people, quietly sitting, watching. Some are calm, some fidgety, all have noticed that the lifts' call buttons only have a down arrow and that the pointer on the dial above each door moves very slowly until it reaches three o'clock and the door opens, but very, very quickly back the other way to the point at which it stops – somewhere different every time.

The only people you ever see emerging from the lifts are the bell boys. They walk from the doors to the front of the chairs and point, and nod, and escort a nervous patient to the doors, walking strangely (the bell boys, not the patients) as if their legs weren't jointed in the right places. You get the impression that they never point directly at anybody, but, every time two patients start to stand up together, one always sits down very quickly, looking very relieved.

A neighbour turns to you and whispers with a profound air of authority – somewhat like a war veteran who seems far too sane to be saying such crazy things – or like a drunk who grabs you in the street and almost convinces you, until you realise that something does not compute. "They take them downstairs," he says. "Downstairs to talk to their boss. The patients' boss, not the bell boys'."

"Patients?" you ask, worried to have a crazy whispering guy confirming what you'd been thinking yourself.

"Yeah, patients, customers, whatever. More applicants really. Applicants is better. You see how they're nervous – the applicants, not the bell boys – you know why they're nervous? No? They're nervous because they know they have to go downstairs and convince their boss to let them stay. They're trying to remember everything they've ever done for their boss, what went right, what credit they can claim, what lies they can slip past, what excuses they need to make – why they deserve to stay – they have to convince their boss to let them stay. It's why they're here. They shouldn't be nervous though, once they get in the lifts, they're guaranteed the position they've worked for, what they deserve. There's no need to grovel and beg, but they all do."

You're just about to ask him how he knows all this, when a bell boy shambles over, points and nods. Your neighbour stands up, turns to you and says, "Gotta go, nice meeting ya, funny how it's never empty in here." and then shuffles over to the lifts becoming more and more agitated and reluctant as he goes.

You look around and glance around behind you – the place is full, at least as full as when you arrived, if not fuller, but suddenly the strangest thing you know is that you don't know how you got there, you can't remember your journey, in fact, you're reasonably certain that you couldn't have come all this way (where are you again?) just to beg for a lousy job it seems you'd get anyway. As you try to work out what exactly the hell is going on, a bell boy approaches and you feel yourself standing up. You look around desperately, but all the chairs around you are filled with people resolutely sitting and just-as-desperately avoiding eye contact. You drag your feet as you follow and suddenly it becomes very important to remember something:

Reasons to stay?
No, that's not it.

Something else you'd rather be doing?
Closer, closer.

Promises made in the heat of the night?
Closer, closer.

A life pact made with your best friend?
Closer, closer.

The arrow hits three o'clock with a dull "PONK!"
Did you leave the gas on?
Closer, closer.

The doors slide open.
No, that's not it either – if only you could think!
Closer, closer.

And then it hits you:
A gust of hot stale air from the lift shaft,
The truth, the question, and the answer,
A hint of fresh air from a door you hadn't noticed before –
right next to the lift. It is open, there are steps beyond it,
steps leading upwards, and you...

A Night on the Outside

Most nights, I go to bed wishing I was dead and cursing myself for a fat, useless idiot. It's been that way for a long time now – the death wish being the default settings on the self-esteem formatted brain-drive. Sometimes, I'm distracted from it by the day or evening I've had and, most of the time, I don't really notice it's there. Unless I'm having a bad day – that's when the only things that calm me down are thoughts of me dying in a variety of ways. If I'm having a really bad day, I'll plan it – my escape route.

I mention the above merely to set the scene for a truly remarkable event which took place this Saturday night.

We'd taken a group of young people from church away for a combination of outdoorsy pursuits and a weekend looking at the subject of the Holy Spirit. After a day's worth of study sessions and activities, we held a small service – during which there was a chance for anybody who wanted to be 'filled with the Holy Spirit'* to be prayed for by the others . In due course, I sat down and was prayed for, and felt nothing.

After the service, we hung around, chatted and drank tea whilst I tried to plan the mini-seminar I was due to be leading in the morning. Eventually, with half a sheet of A4 covered with scribbled ideas, I decided to call it a night. Back at the cabin, I changed, turned out the light and lay down.

---

*Many Christians believe that, when somebody first becomes a
Christian, the Holy Spirit comes and somehow lives in them,
and that it's possible to be 'topped up' with 'Spirit Power'…

As I closed my eyes, I noticed that something was missing: any thought of self harm or suicide or death whatsoever. And more than that: any negative thoughts or feelings about myself were similarly absent. I felt completely peaceful – at ease with myself and life – grateful to have escaped so painlessly. To be fair, I was occasionally aware of the old thoughts trying to creep in, but they seemed to come from a long way off and to be in no way part of what made me 'me'.

I was kind of okay when I noticed that I wasn't getting to sleep – let the insomnia continue if lying in bed is going to feel as good as this! I couldn't even stay cross when the boys came charging into the cabin in high spirits and took their own sweet time quietening down. Even Pete's snoring from the next room seemed less madness-inducing.

So, this is what life on the outside feels like!

Eventually, a not-particularly-fitful doze became sleep for the remainder of the night.

When I woke up, I wanted to die. My glorious escape had only been a night on remand, but no less glorious for that.

The Party

There is a man in the street, outside a party. The sounds of the party are spilling out and washing over him: laughter, glasses clinking, music, conversation – the general sounds of revelry. The only light in the street comes from the party and the man is lit dimly as most of the light is blocked by people inside, enjoying themselves and casting shadows onto the street. In this dim light, the man casts a dimmer shadow as he kneels at the foot of a broken lamp post, screaming.

He has been screaming for a long time and is utterly alone – just the man and his scream. He cannot remember a time when he hasn't been screaming. Sometimes he curls up in a ball and sleeps and, for a while, there is blessed silence but he is unaware of this – he is screaming as he falls asleep and the sound of his screams wakes him.

The party has been going on a long time and he would love to go inside – but he can't stop screaming and he knows this would disturb the others and he doesn't know how to stop.

One day, he feels something different. He feels an arm across his shoulders and the warmth of somebody kneeling next to him. He has no more idea of how long this stranger has been holding him than he has of how long he has been screaming. As the stranger holds him, the man notices that his screaming is becoming less intense and is giving way to sobs and tears and sniffles.

The stranger carries on holding him.

Eventually, the man is silent. He has no more tears, no more pain, no more screaming. "Come inside," says the stranger. The man is reluctant: his clothes are dirty, his trousers torn at the knees from years of kneeling; he can't face the people inside, his voice is hoarse. It's all too much for him – too soon. "Don't worry," says the stranger. "Come in the kitchen and we'll have a cup of tea."

Together, they stand up, and, holding each other, they walk shakily inside.

Word: *Bellwether* (n. c. 1900):

Theoretical scale of measurement used by Henry Poincaré in early Chaos Theory to standardise the measurement of the severity of violent storms caused halfway round the globe by seemingly insignificant actions here. A Force 10 Hurricane would previously have been accorded a score of 5.6 butterflies, but under the new scale, Force 10 would be accorded $1\mu BW$. The old church bell used to create the scale is kept (for safety's sake) securely under lock and key in a basement of the Bureau International des Poids et Mesures in Sèvres, France.

Reporting In

Hi, this is the Monster in Tim's Head again. Thank you all so much for the well wishes following my sudden absence – it truly has made my heart grow fonder – I had been granted an extended holiday for all the good work I'd been doing. Management thought we could afford to leave the subject alone with his thoughts for a good long while.

It turns out that wasn't such a good idea, something for which I accept no responsibility whatsoever.

But I'm back. And, boy, do I have my work cut out for me!

Last night, after a very good day (for him), Tim went home feeling a trifle low – a perfectly natural condition after a long and fun day – and with just a few whispers I had him weakly contemplating suicide again; it was almost just like the good old days, as if I'd never left. It was wonderful: watching him lying there, struggling, as if his 'newly found freedom' had been torn from him, and wondering if he ever would have a chance at being 'normal'. It was after a couple of hours of this that I made my fatal mistake:

"You've always been this way, and you always will." I whispered – a gem that had worked wonders in the past. Nobody told me that he'd woken up in my absence!

I heard him say, "Don't be silly," Whether this was to himself or to me I'll never know. "Don't be daft, you've had a month and a half without any of this bullshit!" And just like that, I lost him.

I should never have accepted the generous holiday offer in its entirety. So much has unravelled and it's going to be a while before things are back to normal. As ever, your kind thoughts are much appreciated.

Yours,
TMiTH

A Short Christmas Communion Service

- **Welcome**

- **Introduction**

- **Today's Gospel Reading:**
   (Luke 1:46-55)

   In those days Mary set out and went with haste to a
   Judean town in the hill country, where she entered the
   house of Zechariah and greeted Elizabeth. When
   Elizabeth heard Mary's greeting, the child leaped in
   her womb. And Elizabeth was filled with the Holy
   Spirit and exclaimed with a loud cry, "Blessed are you
   among women, and blessed is the fruit of your womb.
   And why has this happened to me, that the mother of
   my Lord comes to me? For as soon as I heard the
   sound of your greeting, the child in my womb leaped
   for joy. And blessed is she who believed that there
   would be a fulfilment of what was spoken to her by
   the Lord."

   And Mary said,

   "My soul magnifies the Lord,
      and my spirit rejoices in God my Saviour,
   for he has looked with favour on the lowliness of his
   servant.
      Surely, from now on all generations will call me

blessed;
for the Mighty One has done great things for me,
    and holy is his name.
His mercy is for those who fear him
    from generation to generation.
He has shown strength with his arm;
    he has scattered the proud in the thoughts of their
hearts.
He has brought down the powerful from their
thrones,
    and lifted up the lowly;
he has filled the hungry with good things,
    and sent the rich away empty.
He has helped his servant Israel,
    in remembrance of his mercy,
according to the promise he made to our ancestors,
    to Abraham and to his descendants forever."

- A prayer of response:

(we all say together:)
Glory to the Father, and to the Son, and to the Holy Spirit:
    as it was in the beginning, is now, and will be for ever.
Amen.

- Prayers for other people:

A chance for us to pray for the church and the world

The Communion Part of the Service

- Statement of belief:
We take it in turn to say one thing we love about Jesus

- Prayers of blessing for the bread and wine:
Whoever is leading the service will break the bread and say thank you to God for it and ask him to bless it, and then hold up the cup, say thanks to God, and ask him to bless the wine.

- The distribution:
We break a bit from the loaf and give it to the person on our **left** and say these (or similar) words: "The body of Christ, broken for you." then pass the loaf to the person on our **right**.
We pass the cup to the person on our **left** and say these (or similar) words: "The blood of Christ, shed for you."

- A thank you prayer:
(we all say together:)
We thank you Lord, that you have fed us with this sacrament*, united us with Jesus, and given us a glimpse of the feast in heaven which you have prepared for the whole world.

---

*sacrament: a physical act, in which God is believed to be especially present and knowable.

- A prayer of blessing:

(we all say to one another:)
The Lord bless you and keep you
The Lord make his face to shine upon you,
and be gracious unto you
The Lord lift up the light of his
countenance upon you and give you peace
Amen

- The sending out:

(Whoever is leading the service says:)
Go in peace, to love and serve the Lord
(We all say:)
In the name of Christ. Amen.

Ash Wednesday Meditation:
Welcome to the Season of Bright Sadness

You will need:

- A copy of Steve Turner's poem, *The Cast of Christmas Reassembles for Easter.* (It can be found at the following website: http://www.poemhunter.com/poem/the-cast-of-christmas-reassembles-for-easter/) and a volunteer to read it without being prompted once the group has settled down and is ready to begin
- One or two large candles
- A large heat proof tray
- A copy of the song *Mercy* by The Gena Rowlands Band from their *Flesh and Spirits* album (available via amazon or downloadable through i-tunes) and some means of playing it back
- Several strips of paper about 10cm x 1cm
- Pencils
- Enough prayer cards (cut from a copy of the next page) to give to everybody who will be there
- A copy of the leader's script/notes

Before you begin:

- Arrange the candles on the heat proof tray so that they are as spread out as possible with the prayer cards scattered around them
- Place a pencil and paper strip on each chair – it helps to have these already in place so the flow of the meditation isn't interrupted by the handing out of the pencils
- Light the candles

Lord God,
we have sinned against you;
we have done evil in your sight.
We are sorry and repent.
Have mercy on us according to
your love.
Wash away our wrongdoing and
cleanse us from our sin.
Renew a right spirit within us
and restore us to the joy of your
salvation,
through Jesus Christ our Lord.
            Amen.

Lord God,
we have sinned against you;
we have done evil in your sight.
We are sorry and repent.
Have mercy on us according to your
love.
Wash away our wrongdoing and
cleanse us from our sin.
Renew a right spirit within us
and restore us to the joy of your
salvation,
through Jesus Christ our Lord.
            Amen.

Lord God,
we have sinned against you;
we have done evil in your sight.
We are sorry and repent.
Have mercy on us according to
your love.
Wash away our wrongdoing and
cleanse us from our sin.
Renew a right spirit within us
and restore us to the joy of your
salvation,
through Jesus Christ our Lord.
            Amen.

Lord God,
we have sinned against you;
we have done evil in your sight.
We are sorry and repent.
Have mercy on us according to your
love.
Wash away our wrongdoing and
cleanse us from our sin.
Renew a right spirit within us
and restore us to the joy of your
salvation,
through Jesus Christ our Lord.
            Amen.

Lord God,
we have sinned against you;
we have done evil in your sight.
We are sorry and repent.
Have mercy on us according to
your love.
Wash away our wrongdoing and
cleanse us from our sin.
Renew a right spirit within us
and restore us to the joy of your
salvation,
through Jesus Christ our Lord.
            Amen.

Lord God,
we have sinned against you;
we have done evil in your sight.
We are sorry and repent.
Have mercy on us according to your
love.
Wash away our wrongdoing and
cleanse us from our sin.
Renew a right spirit within us
and restore us to the joy of your
salvation,
through Jesus Christ our Lord.
            Amen.

Ash Wednesday Meditation – Leader's Script/Notes

\<Your volunteer reads the Steve Turner Poem\>

Introduction:
I've begun with a poem contrasting the feasts to which the seasons of Lent and Advent lead up, because I think they are two sides of the same coin and you can't have one without the other:

Long ago, both were simply called 'Lent', 'Advent' being a more recent name for the pre-Christmas season.

The liturgical colour for both seasons is purple – symbolic of not only pain, suffering, mourning and penitence, but also royalty.

Advent looks forward to the coming life (and second coming) of Jesus, whilst Lent looks towards his death (and resurrection).

One is a time of joyful preparation and decoration, and the other, of penitent self-examination and purification.

Which brings us to today.

Ash Wednesday is the first day of Lent, the season leading up to the trials and disappointment of Holy Week, and the joy and confusion of Easter.

It takes its name from the traditional practice of putting

ashes on our foreheads as a sign of mourning and repentance – a slightly ritualised form of the biblical wearing of sack-cloth and ashes.

Repentance is the continual act of turning away **from** what we know to be wrong and of turning **towards** that which we know to be right.

As the song [Gena Rowlands Band; Mercy] plays, think of something that you need to turn away from and write it down on the slip of paper which was on your chair. Then, when you feel ready, light the paper in the flame of one of the candles and watch as the smoke rises and the ash falls to the trays and the *thing* disappears, leaving behind only the light of the candle flame.

Feel free to watch the candle flames for a while, and before you go back to your seat, please take a prayer card from around the candles.

<play the song>

Final prayer
<once everybody has returned to their seat>

We all say together the prayer on the cards:

Lord God,
we have sinned against you;
we have done evil in your sight.
We are sorry and repent.
Have mercy on us according to your love.

Wash away our wrongdoing and cleanse us from our sin.
Renew a right spirit within us
and restore us to the joy of your salvation,
through Jesus Christ our Lord.
            Amen.

Martha and Mary

This was written for a group of eighteen 11-14 year olds, split into three groups, but will work with smaller numbers and older participants. It takes about an hour and a half to run. We started with notices and a recap of the previous sessions in the series, followed by a game. After the game, the session ran uninterrupted as described.

You will need:

- At least three leaders – one for each of the stations
- Copies of the notes for each of the leaders
- A schedule of the day's session (I've included the one we used as a guide) – enough copies to give to each leader
- Envelopes, pens, paper
- A flip chart and marker pens
- A copy of the bible verses which will be used (http://www.biblegateway.com/ is an invaluable resource)
- Enough copies of the Martha and Mary prayer to leave for people to take away from the response parts of stations 1 and 2

Session Schedule (example)

Introduction and Notices

Game

Read the Bible Bits (Luke 10:38-42; John 11:1-3, 11:17-28, 11:29-32 12:1-3)

Split into groups to go round 'stations'

Feedback after 'stations'

Response time

Leader's Script

After Game #1:

Introduce by explaining the interesting facts:
- The Catholics identify Mary as being the same person as Mary Magdalene, but most other Christian traditions don't
- The Orthodox Church identify Mary and Martha as being two of the women who went to anoint Jesus' body at the tomb
- Many mentions of visits to Bethany throughout the gospels so likely that Jesus would be a regular visitor to M&M

Get volunteers to read the following (hand out print outs of passages to the volunteers):
Luke 10:38-42 (service vs. sitting)
John 11v1-3 (Lazarus sick, mention of oil onto feet)
John 11v17-28 (Meeting Martha)
John 11v29-32 (Meeting Mary)
John 12v1-3 (anointing of Jesus by Mary)

Explain about the stations:

You'll be split into three groups, and move around the stations in your groups, taking five (it worked out at closer to seven) minutes or so at each. Once you've completed all three, we'll get back together in a large group and feedback.

Station 1:   Good Friends and a Packet of Crisps
Station 2:   The Drama of Busy vs. Worthwhile
Station 3:   Cause of Upset

Split them into groups and set them off

Collect everybody back together.

Feedback leading to discussion from each of the stations in order.

Ask everybody to think about which area of the stories they connected most with. Explain that they should go back to that area and look at the responses on the tables quietly and in their own time.

Station 1:
Good Friends and a Packet of Crisps (Safe Places)

(Use flip chart sheets and marker pens)

Jesus went to stay with Martha and Mary and they looked after him, and in Mary's anointing of him Mary took this further (Jesus said that it was preparing him for his burial). The orthodox tradition carries this on further still with them going to take care of his body on Easter Sunday...

- Is there anywhere that you go to get looked after, and maybe recharge your batteries?
- When you're in these places, which is more important – talking to people, or being fed?
- Do you provide a safe place to relax for anybody?
- Do you tend to bustle and busy about, or spend quality time with your friends?
- What's your favourite bit about being hospitable?
- How do you think Jesus felt about the care he received from Martha and Mary?
- What do you think Jesus would say if you were entertaining (in a looking after kind of way, not tap-dancing whilst wearing a blindfold and balancing a bowl of trifle on your head kind of way) him?

During the feedback,
get a spokesman for each group to go over what they've got on the flip charts – maybe not direct questions and answers, but anything which came across as important during the discussions.

Station 2:
The Drama of Busy vs. Worthwhile

Get the group to come up with a short drama of a time from their life when either they've been too busy and missed something important,

or
when they've been forced away from something important by somebody else's busy-ness.

Get them to realise at which point in the story things went wrong, and come up with an alternative, better ending. If that's going to take too much time, or complicate things too much, don't worry.

I'd imagine that they'll all try to go for something like "I was watching the telly and Mum made me wash up." But try to get each group to do something different.

During the feedback,
get them to act out the initial sketch and ask the other two groups where they'd change the story and why and if appropriate get the group to re-enact the sketch with the alternative ending.

Station 3:
Cause of Upset

(It really helps to have the passages printed and ready for this bit)

Read John 11:1-6, 20-22 & 32

- Would you have reacted in a similar way to the girls in their situation (especially given that Jesus took his time responding to their message)?
- Is it all right for Martha and Mary to be angry/tetchy with Jesus "If you'd been here, this wouldn't have happened!"?
- Are there any bits of your life where you think "If God had been here, then none of this would have happened and I wouldn't be in this crappy mess."?
- Do you have the same kind of faith as Martha in Verse 22?

Read John 11:33-35

- Is it surprising that Jesus wept only after seeing the effect that Lazarus's death had on his friends?
- What do you think of the idea of Jesus being upset?
- How do you think Jesus responds to the effect that any of the situations we just mentioned have on you?

Read John 11:41-44

- Clearly it's a good thing that Lazarus was brought back from the dead, but does his having come back to life nullify (make meaningless) the anger and pain of Mary and Martha before that?

- Does it mean that Jesus was upset for no good reason?
- Is there anything in your life that you're still waiting for God to act on?

During the feedback,

mention briefly that it's okay to be upset with or angry with God (although some may not agree), and ask members of each group to mention anything of interest.

Station 1: The Response

Either:

Write a short thank you note to people who've shown you hospitality, mention that you've been looking at Mary and Martha today and that, in the same way that Jesus would have appreciated their hospitality, you appreciate theirs.

Or

Think of ways you can be hospitable to your friends over the coming week. Choose one, plan it out now, and put it into action this week. Tell one of the leaders about it at the next session.

And

Take away a copy of the prayer below to read through, think about and pray during the week:

O God, heavenly Father, whose Son Jesus Christ enjoyed rest and refreshment in the home of Mary and Martha of Bethany: Give us the will to love you, open our hearts to hear you, and strengthen our hands to serve you in others for his sake; who lives and reigns with you and the Holy Spirit, now and for ever.

Station 2: The Response

Think about what's worthwhile in your day-to-day life and what's merely busy-ness. It might be helpful to make a list of the things which take up your time and circling the ones you believe are important.

Ask God to help you make the right choices throughout the week.

Take away a copy of the prayer below to read through, think about and pray during the week:

O God, heavenly Father, whose Son Jesus Christ enjoyed rest and refreshment in the home of Mary and Martha of Bethany: Give us the will to love you, open our hearts to hear you, and strengthen our hands to serve you in others for his sake; who lives and reigns with you and the Holy Spirit, now and for ever.

Station 3: The Response

Christians believe that, like with the raising of Lazarus, all circumstances, no matter how rotten, can be redeemed by God. This doesn't lessen the awfulness of bad situations, but provides an element of hope which can help us move forward.

It's okay to be in the middle of events which seem totally cut off from God – it may be a very long time before Jesus raises your 'Lazarus'.

If there's something you're angry with God about or that you're waiting to change in a dramatic way, write about it (what's going on, how it makes you feel, and what for you would be the ideal outcome) and seal it in one of the envelopes. Write today's date and your name on the envelope and leave it on the table. One of the leaders will (without opening the envelope) regularly pray for you and for God to noticeably work in your circumstances. If things change, come and ask for the envelope back.

Ask God to show you that Jesus is with you and affected by the things that happen to you, and that no matter how dark things may seem that there is hope.

O God, heavenly Father, whose Son Jesus Christ enjoyed rest and refreshment in the home of Mary and Martha of Bethany: Give us the will to love you, open our hearts to hear you, and strengthen our hands to serve you in others for his sake; who lives and reigns with you and the Holy Spirit, now and for ever.

O God, heavenly Father, whose Son Jesus Christ enjoyed rest and refreshment in the home of Mary and Martha of Bethany: Give us the will to love you, open our hearts to hear you, and strengthen our hands to serve you in others for his sake; who lives and reigns with you and the Holy Spirit, now and for ever.

O God, heavenly Father, whose Son Jesus Christ enjoyed rest and refreshment in the home of Mary and Martha of Bethany: Give us the will to love you, open our hearts to hear you, and strengthen our hands to serve you in others for his sake; who lives and reigns with you and the Holy Spirit, now and for ever.

O God, heavenly Father, whose Son Jesus Christ enjoyed rest and refreshment in the home of Mary and Martha of Bethany: Give us the will to love you, open our hearts to hear you, and strengthen our hands to serve you in others for his sake; who lives and reigns with you and the Holy Spirit, now and for ever.

O God, heavenly Father, whose Son Jesus Christ enjoyed rest and refreshment in the home of Mary and Martha of Bethany: Give us the will to love you, open our hearts to hear you, and strengthen our hands to serve you in others for his sake; who lives and reigns with you and the Holy Spirit, now and for ever.

O God, heavenly Father, whose Son Jesus Christ enjoyed rest and refreshment in the home of Mary and Martha of Bethany: Give us the will to love you, open our hearts to hear you, and strengthen our hands to serve you in others for his sake; who lives and reigns with you and the Holy Spirit, now and for ever.

About the Author

Tim Hardy is apparently 'an all round good egg': he works in a library, volunteers with the youngsters at church and helps old ladies cross the road (whether they want to or not).

In his spare time, he has been known to write short stories and poems – which he imagines you'd count as a good thing, since you would otherwise be holding fifty blank pages in a very pretty cover. Of course, he's happy to admit that you might prefer the blank pages after all.

He is very glad to have more-or-less permanently seen the back of the monster in his head, and wishes it a long and unhealthy absence.

What else? Oh, one of his legs is slightly longer than the other. Curiously, they both reach the ground.

Secretly, Tim Hardy *quite* likes *most* pedants.

In early 2007, he took part in a 'Blogathon' - writing on a subject chosen by a sponsor every half hour for twenty four hours. A small selection of the more coherent pieces follows.

Where Do All the Lost Socks Go?
- for Miss Erica Jaques

I've never had the experience of losing a sock. I imagine they run away to the city to seek their fortune, and either end up dead in a ditch before they're even three miles from home, hook up with a homeless glove they meet along the way (and, if they're traditional, visit Gretna Green, get hitched by the blacksmith, and go on to raise a family of little millinery), sleep rough in shop doorways or hostels, or (if they're lucky) they find somebody who'll turn them into a monkey and go on to find fame and fortune. A fortunate few turn up at a later date with either a smug grin or a trace of fear in their eyes that says they're haunted by memories of such horror as we can only imagine.

Physics
- for Miss Hannah Hardy

Physics and Theology are the only two proper sciences and Mathematics is the language of Physics.

Chemistry is merely physics at an atomic/molecular level.

Biology is merely chemistry scaled up a bit.

So, everything is Physics or Theology.

I guess if Theology is the 'Queen of the Sciences' then Physics must be the King.

I studied Physics at university for two and half years, and now I work in a library which deals with Religious Studies and Theology, I guess I'm just a royalist.

But enough about me, this is meant to be about physics - it is the study of everything that can be measured, from the tiniest of tiniest things, to the biggest of biggest and everything in between; sound, colour, shape, liquids, solids, gases, plasma, everything.

Physicists are renowned for their crazy hair, for example, me when I was a physicist, The Prof. from the *Back to the Future* films and Einstein - crazy hair all round, I think I've picked a representative sample there.

And that's all there is to know about Physics.

The History of Organic Farming in Switzerland
for - Mr James 'Fiendish' Milne

The Swiss have been growing human organs for years now. They supply a growing area of the black market which grew up after the end of the second world war.

It all started when a cuckoo-clock maker called Hans(one of the many traditional manufacturing immigrants from the coal-starved UK) realised that the fertile Tobleroney Alpen slopes were perfect for organ farming. He started with a basic graft of human skin onto a solitary cell, on the western Swiss Bank* and pretty soon he produced a runner (I hope you appreciate botanic-human punnery here, it's just about killing me). Within a couple of years, he had a whole team of Olympic athletes.

And the rest, as they say, is history.

*Hans wasn't his real name, but it's all historians could make out of the ten digit code that was used to identify his account.

Eschatology
- for the Revd Canon Richard Bryant

This is a big word - and as I am a Tim of very little brain and long words confuse me I had to look it up. The dictionary says:
the method or skill of extricating oneself from handcuffs, chains, etc., as of a magician or other performer.
But I'm sure that this can't be what a senior(ish) clergyman in the Church of England would want me to write about, although...
Okay, it's really the study of the "End Times" - this being one of the more titularly self explanatory doctrines of the church - it's all to do with what happens during the times at the end.
Not to be confused with Eschertology - where, no matter how many stairs you climb, you always find yourself back where you started, with no end in sight.
Which is loosely translated (by some smart alecs) as "the recent history of the church - from which few people want to escape." Which brings us back to...